1005-12

2.50

# A Little

# Cookbook

## Terry Tan

### ILLUSTRATED BY SUSAN DRAY

Peter G. Schmidt Library
Tumwater, Washington

D0429561

First published in 1990 by
The Appletree Press Ltd, 7 James Street South,
Belfast BT2 8DL.
Copyright © 1990 The Appletree Press, Ltd. Illustrations ©
1990 Susan Dray used under Exclusive License to
The Appletree Press, Ltd.
Printed in Hong Kong. All rights reserved.
No part of this publication may be
reproduced or transmitted in any form
or by means, electronic or mechanical,
photocopying, recording or any information
and retrieval system, without permission in
writing from the publisher

First published in the United States in 1990
by Chronicle Books, 275 Fifth Street,
San Francisco, CA 94103

ISBN: 0-87701-798-0

9 8 7 6 5 4 3 2 1

# Introduction

While Chinese cuisine is universally popular, it has the undeserved reputation of being intimidating. Those 'mystifying sauces' are easily available in stores. As for methods and utensils, this book will de-mystify them. The Ying Yang philosophy that permeates Chinese life is evident in its cuisine, giving a balance of opposite elements – dark and light, soft and crunchy, sweet and sour. The result should be a feeling of well-being after a meal. No two Chinese chefs ever cook the same dish the same way; each creates his own flavors. Whether attempting an imperial Peking Duck or humble peasant stew, approach it with a sense of adventure and boldness. It's a matter of trial and a few errors before you know the perfect harmony between ginger and sesame oil, plum sauce and vinegar, soy sauce and garlic, noodles and beansprouts and the endless permutations therein. A Chinese meal for four consists of two or three dishes served with rice. All dishes will serve two or more if the meal includes other dishes, unless otherwise indicated. A meal for four can easily be stretched by serving more rice.

## A note on measures

Spoon measurements are level except where otherwise indicated. Seasonings can of course be adjusted according to taste. Recipes are for four.

# Savory Tossed Chicken Noodles

Bread is not truly a part of Chinese cuisine and breakfast is really pot luck. Mostly a simplified version of lunch or dinner, it draws from a wide range of single-portion rice and noodle-based dishes. 4 oz noodles is ample for one.

---

4 oz dry egg noodles
3 tbsp vegetable oil
6 oz chicken breast
1 stalk celery
2 tbsp dark soy sauce
1/2 tsp ground black pepper
1 cup water
1 chicken stock cube
spring onions, chopped

---

Cook noodles to packet instructions. Drain and loosen strands. Slice chicken into thin strips. Slice celery on the diagonal 3/4 in wide. Heat oil in wok or frying pan until smoking and add chicken, stirring vigorously until meat turns opaque. Add celery, soy sauce, pepper, water, and stock cube. When this boils, add noodles and stir well, raking strands with a fork. Cook for 2 minutes and serve garnished with chopped spring onions. Typically, left over chicken will be used.

# Braised Rice Noodles

Chinese noodles are made from wheat, rice, or mung bean flour. Sold dry, or occasionally fresh in specialty stores, they need only be boiled or soaked till soft. Wheat noodles expand to roughly twice their bulk but rice and mung bean noodles do not.

---

8 oz rice noodles
I clove garlic, crushed
2 tbsp vegetable oil
3 tbsp oyster sauce
10 fl oz water
1/2 cup beansprouts
3 oz raw shrimp
3 oz cleaned squid
1/2 tsp pepper
fresh coriander or spring onions, chopped

---

Cook noodles to packet instructions adding 2 tbsp oil when boiling to prevent sticking. Drain. Clean and devein shrimps. Cut squid into 1/2 in rings or 1 in squares if large. Fry garlic in hot oil till light brown. Add oyster sauce and water and bring to a boil. Add shrimps and squid and cook for 1 minute. Add all other ingredients and stir well for about 2 minutes. Serve garnished with fresh coriander or chopped spring onions.

# Yangzhou Jewel Rice

"Have you eaten rice?" is the traditional Chinese greeting, explaining its importance to the Chinese. Yangzhou (sometimes spelled Yang Chow) is the Eastern city on the Yang Tze region from which fried rice originated. It is a colorful mix of rice, ham, peas, carrots, and egg, hence the jewel reference.

---

*1 cup long grain rice (enough water to cover 1 in above rice level)*
*4 tbsp oil*
*2 eggs, lightly beaten*
*6 oz cooked ham, cut into ¾ in cubes*
*2 tbsp cooked green peas*
*2 carrots, cubed and blanched*
*1 vegetable stock cube, crumbled*
*spring onions, chopped*

---

Wash rice, add water, and cook covered, over a medium heat for 10-12 minutes, until all water is absorbed. Switch off heat. Stir to loosen and allow to get completely cold. Heat oil and cook eggs until set. Add all other ingredients. Stir well to break up stock cube. Garnish with chopped spring onions.

# Shrimp Dumpling Soup

From ancient times, Chinese people were fond of eating at tea houses. From these came a range of snacks now a permanent feature in most Chinese restaurants. A Dim Sum (literally 'to touch the heart') meal can be two or 200 dishes!

---

20 won ton pastry skins, each 2.5 in
12 oz minced pork
6 oz raw minced prawns
2 tsp cornstarch
2 tbsp sesame oil
1/2 tbsp pepper
2 tbsp light soy sauce
2 oz translucent vermicelli, soaked till soft
30 fl oz water
1 chicken stock cube
fresh coriander or spring onions, chopped

---

Mix pork, prawns, cornstarch, sesame oil, pepper, and soy sauce. Place 2 tsp on each won ton skin, gather up and twist to seal with a little water. Bring water and stock cube to boil. Drop in dumplings and vermicelli, cook for 3 minutes. Adjust seasoning. Garnish with fresh coriander or chopped spring onions.

# Chicken Pancake Rolls

This is another Dim Sum item with more variations than leaves on a tree! Minced pork and cabbage is the classic filling but you can vary with chicken and beansprouts or any shredded leafy vegetable.

*6 spring roll skins 10 in square*
*2 tbsp oil*
*2 cloves garlic, crushed*
*12 oz chicken breast, minced*
*2 cups beansprouts*
*2 tbsp light soy sauce*
*1 tsp pepper*
*oil for deep-frying*
*3 tbsp sesame oil*
*cucumber, sliced*

Heat oil and fry garlic until light brown. Add all other ingredients and stir-fry for 3 minutes until chicken is cooked. Allow to cool. If needed, defrost spring roll skins, keeping them covered with a damp tea towel to prevent cracking while working. Place 2 tbsp of mixture near the edge of skin. Roll over once, fold in sides and roll again to make a firm sausage. Seal edges with a little water and allow to sit for a few minutes. Add sesame oil to deep-fry oil for nutty fragrance. Deep-fry rolls until golden brown and serve with a chili sauce dip and sliced cucumbers.

# Sesame Toast

Though a migrant snack in its use of bread, this is an hors d'oeuvre with lots of savory crunch. Use a pastry cutter to make rounds of bread.

---

*1 sandwich loaf with crust trimmed*
*¾ cup minced pork*
*6 oz raw minced prawns*
*3 eggs, lightly beaten*
*2 tbsp light soy sauce*
*½ tsp pepper*
*⅓ cup sesame seeds*
*oil for deep-frying*

---

Mix pork, prawns and 2 tbsp of beaten egg with soy sauce and pepper. Cut bread into rounds about 1.5 inches in diameter. With a pastry brush, lightly coat each round with egg and spread mixture about ¼ in thick, patting down firmly. You should get between 20 and 24 pieces. Brush with more egg and coat with sesame seeds. Fry a few at a time until golden brown, turning once. Drain on absorbent paper.

# Plum Sauce Chicken

Chinese chefs are masters at making inexpensive ingredients look and taste wonderful. With a little work, humble chicken wings become imperial offerings. All you need is patience, ingenuity, and a sharp knife.

*12 chicken wings, tips removed*
*2 eggs, lightly beaten*
*10 cream crackers, finely crushed*
*oil for deep frying*
*4 tbsp plum sauce*
*2 tbsp hoi sin sauce*
*cucumber rounds*
*pineapple rings*

Cut away thin end of wing joint. Scrape down along the two bones until meat forms a thick ball at the other end. Shape firmly into little lollipops. Remove thin bone leaving thick one as a handle. Roll first in beaten egg and then in crushed crackers. Leave to settle for a few minutes before deep-frying until golden brown. Keep crisp in a warm oven. Serve on rounds of cucumber and pineapple rings with dips of plum and hoi sin sauce.

# Pot Stickers

Legend has it that a forgetful chef burnt a batch of dumplings. His quick-witted son deflected the Emperor's wrath by saying his father had invented a special dish called 'pot stickers' with burnt bottoms. To further mask the fault, he served them with sharp vinegar and ginger sauce.

---

*3 cups plain flour, sifted*
*1 cup warm water*
**Filling**
*1 cup shredded cabbage*
*1 cup minced pork*
*2 tbsp light soy sauce*
*½ tsp pepper*
*2 tbsp sesame oil*
*1 egg, lightly beaten*
*5 tbsp oil for frying*

---

Mix flour with water and knead for 10 minutes until dough comes away from bowl. Rest dough for 20 minutes. Blanch cabbage in boiling water for 2 minutes, drain and mix with other ingredients. Divide dough into 3 parts. Roll each into 10 in lengths. Cut into 10 rings and roll each out into 3 in round. Place 2 tsp of filling in each and shape into half moons, pinching each firmly to seal. Heat oil in a frying pan and lightly brown as many as you can at one time. Add ¾ cup water, cover and cook until the pan is dry and the bottom of each pot sticker is brown. To make the dip, mix 4 tbsp malt vinegar with 2 tbsp soy sauce and 2 tbsp finely shredded ginger.

# Chinese Steamed Bun

This basic Chinese dough mix can also be wrapped around a multitude of fillings for delicious sweet or savory dumplings. A north China staple (no rice is grown in this region) symbolizing plenty, traditionally it is served steamed with savory meat dishes.

*4 cups plain flour, sifted*
*2 tbsp dried yeast*
*2 tsp sugar*
*3 tbsp lukewarm water*
*I cup warm milk*

Mix yeast, sugar, and warm water. Leave in warm place till frothy. Pour this and warm milk into flour. Stir until firm dough is formed. Knead on a floured board for 15 minutes and leave in warm place until dough doubles. Knead for 5 minutes and roll into sausage shape about 1 in in diameter. Cut into 24 rounds and roll out each to 4 in diameter. Fold over and lightly brush with oil. Rest for 20 minutes. Place on a wet cloth on a perforated steamer rack (bamboo is best) and steam for 20 minutes. Allow 1 in space between buns. Serve hot or cold.

# Pork Dumplings

So revered is the dumpling in Chinese cuisine that there is a festival honoring it. They are given as offerings to Taoist deities and after prayers villagers feast on them.

---

*Dumpling dough (see page 20)*
## Filling
*1 lb pork fillet*
## Marinade
*2 tbsp sugar*
*2 tbsp light soy sauce*
*3 tbsp honey*
*2 tbsp hoi sin sauce*

---

Cut pork into strips about 1 in thick. Steep in marinade ingredients for 30 minutes. Roast on a rack for 40 minutes in pre-heated oven at 400°F. Cool and cut into 1/2 in cubed dice. Knead proven dough for 5 minutes and roll into sausage shape about 1 1/2 inches in diameter. Cut into 24 rounds. Flatten each till 4 inches in diameter. Place 1 tbsp filling on each, draw up sides, and twist at top to seal firmly. Steam as for plain dumplings for 20 minutes. Serve hot or cold. Vary the filling with chicken or beef.

# Crab and Sweetcorn Soup

Chinese soups are generally served with a meal so diners may take sips to refresh the palate between mouthfuls. There are herbal soups like those with ginseng reputed to do the libido no end of good! This one is less exciting but very satisfying, especially on a cold winter's evening.

---

1 1/2 cups creamed sweetcorn
1/2 cup crab meat
12 fl oz water
3 tbsp sesame oil
2 tbsp light soy sauce
1/2 tsp pepper
2 eggs
fresh coriander, chopped
croutons

---

Beat eggs lightly and combine all ingredients in a soup pot. Bring to a boil and adjust seasoning to taste. Serve with croutons and chopped fresh coriander. To vary, use diced chicken or shrimps. More egg will give you a thicker, heartier soup.

# Egg Drop Mushroom Soup

Smoky-flavored Chinese dried mushrooms are quite different from field mushrooms. They symbolize prosperity, especially those with fissures on the caps. These 'blossom' mushrooms can be expensive during festive seasons so use field mushrooms instead.

---

*3 cups water*
*I vegetable stock cube*
*6 Chinese mushrooms, soaked in hot water till soft*
*I tbsp shredded ginger*
*4 tbsp Chinese wine (Hsiao Hsing or Hwa Chiu)*
*3 tbsp seasme oil*
*2 eggs, lightly beaten*
*2 tbsp brandy*

---

Bring stock cube and water to a boil. Snip off mushroom stalks and cut each top into strips. Add to stock together with ginger, wine, and sesame oil. As the soup boils pour in beaten egg, gently swirling as you do. Just before serving add brandy.

# Shrimp Fu Yong

To dine off Fu Yong is to augur a smooth path to prosperity, or so say the Chinese. It is also good eating. The classic ingredients are egg and carrot with shrimps or crab.

---

*5 eggs, lightly beaten*
*1 large carrot, grated*
*8 oz raw shrimp or crab meat*
*3 tbsp oil*
*1 tbsp light soy sauce*
*2 spring onions, chopped*
*1 tbsp sesame seeds*
*lettuce leaves*

---

Clean and devein shrimps. Heat oil and fry carrot for 1 minute. Push aside and pour in beaten egg. Stir gently for 2 minutes as you would for scrambled eggs then add shrimps and soy sauce. Continue stirring until shrimps turn pink and Fu Yong is almost dry. Serve with chopped spring onions and sesame seeds sprinkled on top. The Chinese say that 'to eat sesame seeds is to have numerous progeny, a farmer's blessing of many hands to till the soil'. For an amusing starter, the Fu Yong can be wrapped in fresh lettuce leaves.

# Spicy Sichuan Spareribs

There's nothing spare about Chinese ribs, if you can get your butcher to reserve some with plenty of meat on them. Get him to chop them up as you would need a heavy cleaver and some strength to hew through the bone. To make ribs succulent and tender, the trick is to parboil them in their marinade before deep frying.

*2 lbs spareribs, cut into 2 in pieces*
*3 tbsp hoi sin sauce*
*2 tsp Sichuan peppercorns*
*4 tbsp sherry or Chinese wine*
*1/2 tsp five spice powder*
*2 cups water*
*oil for deep frying*

Marinate ribs in all ingredients except water for 1 hour or overnight. Add water and bring to a boil. Cook for 20 minutes until liquid is reduced. Drain and cool. Heat oil until smoking and fry ribs for 2 minutes. Reduce marinade until thick and serve as a side dip. For less oily ribs you can also barbecue after boiling.

# Drunken Chicken

This is believed to be a favorite of the Tang Dynasty Empress Yang Kwei Fei renowned for her beauty and her fondness for a tipple. Traditionally cooked in a clay pot, a Chinese chicken, served whole with its head, represents the Phoenix and rebirth. You wouldn't want to go to your other life headless!

---

*1 chicken, about 3 lb*
*6 tbsp oil*
*1/3 cup Chinese wine or sherry*
*7 cups water*
*4 tbsp light soy sauce*
*2 tbsp shredded ginger*
*4 tbsp sesame oil*
*2 cloves garlic, crushed*

---

Mix 2 tbsp each of soy sauce and wine and rub over chicken. Turn chicken in heated oil until light brown. Transfer to a deep pot with all other ingredients and simmer for 1 1/2 hours. Turn several times and add a little water or wine if necessary. Serve hot or cold with steamed buns. Most Chinese supermarkets sell clay pots. The clay imparts a smoky flavor to the dish and the pot, served straight from the stove, gives an authentic and rustic touch.

# Soy Braised Chicken

You will see this Cantonese specialty hanging in most Chinese restaurants. Done well, it will have a mahogany sheen. Served with a sharp chili dip and plain rice it's positively ambrosial. It's practically a national lunchtime meal.

*1 chicken, about 3 lb*
*4 tbsp oil*
*2 tbsp sugar*
*6 tbsp dark soy sauce*
*1 large knob ginger root, bruised*
*2 tsp salt*
*2 tbsp chopped onion*
*water*

Heat oil and caramelize sugar until it is a dark brown but not burned. Add soy sauce and quickly turn chicken in it until well coated. Add water, ginger, salt, and onion and simmer for 1 hour, turning several times. Cool and cut into pieces. Reduce sauce and serve with chicken. To make a quick chili dip, grind 4 fresh red chilies with 3 cloves of garlic and mix with 4 tbsp malt vinegar and 1 tsp salt.

# Chicken and Cashew Nuts in Yellow Bean Sauce

The epitome of culinary balance in Chinese cuisine, this dish has a perfect blend of texture, shape, color and flavor. It is easy to cook in either a wok or a frying pan.

---

3 tbsp oil
8 oz chicken breast, cubed
2 tbsp yellow bean sauce
I red pepper, diced in ½ in squares
I stalk celery, diced as above
20 cashew nuts
I tsp sugar
2 tbsp sesame oil
5 tbsp water

---

Heat oil and fry chicken for I minute till half cooked. Add yellow bean sauce and stir to blend. Add all other ingredients except water and stir-fry for 2 minutes. Add water, stir, and when mixture thickens remove from wok and serve hot.

# Peking Duck

Aficionados wax lyrical about this splendid dish, even down to the merit of adding ducks' beaks! In Peking, some restaurants are devoted entirely to this dish and some books specify the type of oven and firewood to roast this princely dish. You will still dine with imperial grandeur using a good Aylesbury duckling and store-bought Mandarin pancakes!

---

*1 good sized duckling*
*2 tbsp honey diluted with a little water*
**Accompaniments**
*Mandarin pancakes (store-bought)*
*5 tbsp hoi sin sauce*
*4 stalks spring onions, cut into fine strips 2 in long*
*1 cucumber, skinned, cored, and cut into similar size*

---

Hang duck overnight in a warm place, or on your clothesline in direct sunlight for 3-4 hours until skin is absolutely dry. The secret is to remove as much moisture as possible. A good blast all over with a hair-dryer does the job also. Pre-heat oven for 30 minutes at 400°F. Rub melted honey all over duck and roast on a rack for 40 minutes. Turn heat to medium and roast for a further 30 minutes. Remove duck, leave for 15 minutes. Allowing 4 or 5 pancakes for each person, steam a few at a time for 10 minutes and keep warm. Slice duck skin with a little meat into 2 inch squares. Paint each pancake with a little hoi sin sauce and place a few shreds of spring onions and cucumber in center. Add a piece or two of duck skin and roll up. Most Chinese supermarkets sell pancakes, but tortillas will make a thicker substitute. Traditionally, the meat from the duck carcass will reappear as stir-fried duck with vegetables, and the bones will be boiled with another vegetable for soup.

# Sweet and Sour Pork

'Fire and water, vinegar, pickle, salt, and plums. Fire boils water and the cook orchestrates the harmony equalizing flavors. Then the master eats and his mind is made equable', said a disciple of Confucius, circa 600 BC. It says everything about this famous Chinese export.

---

I lb pork fillet in I in cubes
2 eggs, lightly beaten
cornstarch
oil for deep frying
½ onion, sliced
2 tomatoes, quartered
I small can pineapple chunks, reserve juice
**Sauce**
3 tbsp plum sauce
3 tbsp tomato sauce
5 tbsp pineapple juice
I tsp malt vinegar

---

Roll pork in egg, remove with a slotted spoon and coat with cornstarch. Shake off excess and leave to settle. Deep fry till golden brown and set aside. Heat 3 tbsp oil and fry onions for I minute. Add sauce ingredients, pineapple, and tomatoes and add pork when sizzling. Sauce should just coat pork. Add a little water for a thinner consistency. Serve with rice.

# Braised Pork Belly

Any aversion to fat pork will change when you've tasted this sinfully rich dish. It's simply not the same made with lean pork. Plain steamed buns (see recipe on page 20) make a perfect foil for every juicy drop.

---

2 lb belly pork, cut into 3 or 4 pieces lengthwise
3 cloves garlic, crushed
4 tbsp dark soy sauce
1 tsp five-spice powder
5 tbsp Chinese wine
3 tbsp oil
1 tsp sugar
4 cups water
fresh coriander

---

Marinate pork for an hour in garlic, soy sauce, five-spice powder and wine. Drain and seal well in hot oil. Add water and sugar and simmer for 1 1/2 hours until pork is tender. Drain and slice. Reduce liquid and pour over sliced pork or serve in a gravy boat with steamed buns and fresh coriander.

# Mongolian Lamb Stew

An ancient stew that was called Tung Po mutton by the 11th century Chinese Muslim poet, painter, and epicure of the same name. Sometimes goat meat is used, but lamb will do just as well.

---

*1 lb stewing lamb, trimmed of fat*
*6 oz potatoes, each cut in four*
*4 oz carrots, cut into ½ in chunks*
*2 tbsp soy sauce*
*1 tsp ground ginger*
*1 tsp five-spice powder*
*½ tsp black pepper*
*6 tbsp oil*
*5 tbsp rice wine*

---

Cut lamb into 1 in pieces. Pat dry and seal well in hot oil. Remove lamb from pan, and fry potatoes and carrots for 5 minutes. Remove and set aside. Put lamb and seasoning ingredients in a deep pot and add water to 1 in above ingredients. Bring to a boil and simmer for 2 hours. Add potatoes, carrots, and rice wine 5 minutes before end of cooking time.

# Steamed Sea Bass

This is possibly the most magnificent and easily prepared fish dish. If you cannot get sea bass, use fresh snapper, grouper, or halibut.

*2 lb sea bass, cleaned and gutted but with head left on*
*2 tbsp shredded ginger*
*3 Chinese mushrooms, soaked and cut into strips*
*2 tbsp light soy sauce*
*½ tsp black pepper*
*4 tbsp sherry*
*2 tbsp oil*
*spring onions, chopped*

Score fish diagonally several times almost to the bone. Place on a plate deep enough to contain steamed juices. Press ginger and mushroom strips into crevices. Dribble over soy sauce, oil, peppers and sherry. Cook for 10 minutes in a steamer with a porous lid (bamboo or perforated metal). Sprinkle with chopped spring onions. Any leftover liquid makes a lovely stock base.

# Stir-Fried Prawns and Snow Peas

The southern Chinese say that 'to eat prawns is to augur well for a happy life'. The word for prawns in the Cantonese dialect is 'ha' as in laughter. Since other Chinese words for prawns do not translate similarly, the belief doesn't apply outside this province.

---

*4 tbsp oil*
*12 large fresh prawns, peeled*
*1 tsp sugar*
*4 oz snow peas, topped and tailed*
*1 clove garlic, crushed*
*1 tbsp light soy sauce*
*2 tbsp sesame oil*
*fresh coriander*

---

Marinate prawns in sugar for an hour. Heat oil and fry crushed garlic till light brown. Add prawns and snow peas and fry rapidly over high heat for 1 minute. Add seasoning and stir for another minute. Serve immediately, garnished with sprigs of fresh coriander.

# Steamed Cabbage Rolls

When cabbage is mentioned in Chinese cooking it can mean the Savoy type or the Winter variety, known as Chinese leaf. This recipe refers to the latter, now widely available and with a sweeter taste.

---

*8 cabbage leaves*
*8 oz minced pork*
*6 oz minced raw prawns*
*I tsp salt*
*I tsp cornstarch*
*½ tsp pepper*
*I egg, lightly beaten*
*shallots or garlic, fried*

---

Boil a pot of water and blanch leaves of equal size until soft but not mushy. Drain and set aside. Mix pork, prawns, and seasoning with egg. Taste for seasoning. Place 2 tbsp of mixture on each leaf and roll up firmly. Steam rolls on a plate for 10 minutes. Serve hot with their own juices garnished with fried shallots or garlic.

# The 18 Lohan

The name of this dish, revered by Buddhist vegetarians, refers to the 18 disciples of the Lord Buddha whose Sanskrit name is Lohan. Here are the original 18 ingredients, but anything up to six gives a satisfying result unless you're a purist: Chinese leaf, dry mushrooms, straw mushrooms, hairy mushrooms, cloud ears, white fungus, snow peas, sweet tofu wafers, brown tofu, red dates, gingko nuts, lotus seeds, translucent vermicelli, hair vegetable, lily buds, preserved bean curd, hoi sin sauce, and garlic.

---

6 snow peas, topped and tailed
2 Chinese cabbage leave, slice into 1 in pieces
6 French beans, topped and tailed
6 Chinese mushrooms, soaked till soft and stalks cut off
12 button mushrooms
20 lily buds (golden needles), soaked till soft and hard tips cut off. Tie each into a knot
1 cube preserved red bean curd, mashed
2 tbsp hoi sin sauce
2 tbsp soy sauce
1 tsp pepper
4 tbsp oil
½ pt cup water

---

Heat oil and blend with preserved bean curd. Add hoi sin sauce and stir for 1 minute. Drain and dry vegetables and add to all other ingredients except water and stir. Add water and cook over high heat, stirring constantly until thick. This dish tastes even better the next day.

# Almond Lychee Surprise

It's a fallacy to think Chinese do not have a sweet tooth. Desserts are not usually served after a meal but rather as in-between snacks. In fact, sugar is revered and the icon of the kitchen diety is always smeared with sugar water so that he will give good reports in heaven about the household!

---

2 packets unflavored gelatin (each about 3 oz)
2 cups water
5 tbsp sugar
1 cup milk
1 tbsp almond essence
1 large can lychees

---

Stir gelatin in half the water and sugar until dissolved. Boil the remaining water and pour into gelatin mixture. Stir until mixture is clear. Blend milk with almond essence and add to mixture. Pour into jelly mold and refrigerate when cool. To serve, either arrange lychees around whole jelly or cut up and serve in individual dishes. Any canned fruit can be used.

# Golden Bites

Butter is rarely, if ever, used in Chinese desserts and I suspect this pudding came to China by way of Far East migrants who enjoyed imported New Zealand butter.

---

## Pastry
*¼ cup butter*
*¼ cup lard*
*1 egg*
*6 tbsp sugar*
*2 cups sifted flour*

## Filling
*4 large eggs, half the white discarded*
*1½ cups milk*
*1 cup sugar*

---

Cream butter with lard and add egg and sugar. Beat well and add flour. Stir till dough is firm. Knead for 10 minutes and set aside. Beat eggs until blended but not frothy. Add sugar and milk and stir over a bowl of warm water. Leave for 15 minutes. Separate dough into 20 balls and press each into a shallow ramekin to form a tart shell, making sure thickness is even. Fill each with egg mixture and bake in pre-heated oven at 300°F, for 40 minutes. Cool and unmold.

# Goreng Pisang

This is an exotic way to treat bananas and it's practically a national snack among migrant populations in Southeast Asia who serve it with scoops of coconut or mango ice cream.

---

*8 bananas, peeled*
*½ cup self-rising flour*
*½ cup rice flour*
*1 tbsp cornstarch*
*1 cup water*
*½ tsp salt*
*4 tbsp fine brown sugar*
*oil for deep frying*

---

Slice each banana lengthwise into two. Sift flours and add to water. Stir until consistency of cream. Add salt. Heat oil and, when smoking, dip each piece of banana in batter. Shake off excess and lower into hot oil. Fry until golden brown and roll in brown sugar. Serve with ice cream.

# Index